VIILI PERPETUAL, NO-COOK, HOMEMADE YOGURT

Caleb Warnock

FAMILIUS

Published by Familius LLC, www.familius.com

Familius books are available at special discounts for bulk purchases for sales promotions or for family or corporate use. Special editions, including personalized covers, excerpts of existing books, or books with corporate logos, can be created in large quantities for special needs. For more information, contact Premium Sales at 559-876-2170 or email orders@familius.com.

Library of Congress Cataloging-in-Publication Data
2015956717

ISBN: 9781942934516
eISBN: 9781944822347
Printed in the United States of America

Edited by Liza Hagerman
Cover design by David Miles
Book design by David Miles and Maggie Wickes

10 9 8 7 6 5 4 3 2 1
First Edition

DISCOVER THE LONG-LOST SKILLS OF SELF-RELIANCE

My name is Caleb Warnock, and I've been working for years to learn how to return to forgotten skills, the skills of our ancestors. As our world becomes increasingly unstable, self-reliance becomes invaluable. Throughout this series, *The Backyard Renaissance*, I will share with you the lost skills of self-sufficiency and healthy living. Come with me and other do-it-yourself experimenters, and rediscover the joys and success of simple self-reliance.

CONTENTS

PART I

VIILI 101

iili yogurt is the world's only homemade yogurt that requires no cooking. Beloved in Finland for centuries, viili is easy to make, full of natural probiotic health, and deliciously creamy! Viili yogurt is also perpetual, meaning that once you have a "starter," you can make the yogurt for years to come. This book will tell you how to get a starter, explain the history of viili, give you detailed instructions with questions and answers, and introduce recipes ranging from homemade yogurt cheese to pancakes and waffles, smoothies, dinner entrées, and more!

Welcome to the world's simplest, most honest, healthy homemade yogurt!

CALEB'S INTRODUCTION TO VIILI

O ne summer afternoon, I was sitting in the kitchen of my friend Linda when she casually pulled some homemade yogurt out of her fridge. "I'm sending this home with you so you can start making your own yogurt," she said.

Linda is a widower who calls herself my "adoptive mother," and the story of how we met became a bit famous after I published it in my *More Forgotten Skills* book.[1] At our first meeting, Linda and I got into a bit of a tiff during a speech I was giving. Afterward, she offered me some of the rarest beans in the world, and since that day, we have been friends. She has taught me to use milk kefir and water kefir, taught me how to sprout "sunflower lettuce" in winter, and introduced me to her rare strawberries. We have compared our greenhouses and swapped plants, and she taught me how to use a thermal oven and the pioneer method for cellaring winter apples. My "adoptive mother" is a treasure trove of homestead wisdom.

On this particular day, I was sitting in her kitchen as we talked about her stevia plants, a sugary green herb she was growing from seeds she got from me. When she went to her fridge to get me a yogurt starter, it was a stealth attack—she had offered me a starter for her yogurt culture several times before, but I had always said no. I was already keeping cultures of natural yeast and two kinds of kefirs, and I wasn't sure I wanted to add another "pet" to my collection. After all, cultures need occasional attention because they are living creatures. (More on that in a moment.)

This time, Linda didn't ask me if I wanted a yogurt starter—she just gave me one. "It's so easy," she said. "All you do is put the starter in a mason jar, add milk, and leave it on your kitchen counter overnight until it forms yogurt."

I was skeptical.

At our house, we were no strangers to homemade yogurt. My wife, Charmayne, and I have a little yogurt-making machine that heats yogurt to the correct temperature for hours, gently cooking it in the traditional way. We had used yogurt from the grocery store as our starter, but it only lasted a few uses before it was no good. The whole process took more time, attention, and counter space than it was worth, and the yogurt cooker had sat in a closet, unused, for years.

In her kitchen, as Linda handed me the yogurt culture in a pint glass jar, she could see the doubt in my eyes. "Just do it," she said. "You're going to love it."

If I say that boy, oh boy, was she right—we do love the culture of viili Finnish yogurt that she gifted us—it would be an understatement.

Notes

1. *Caleb Warnock,* More Forgotten Skills of Self-Sufficiency *(Springville, UT: Cedar Fort, Inc., 2014).*

WHAT IS ViiLi?

efore the invention of modern grocery stores (approximately after World War II), yogurt was commonly homemade using a starter culture.[1] A starter is simply a collection of beneficial bacteria that when fed milk (in the case of yogurt) turn the milk into yogurt. This kind of traditional yogurt is sometimes called "yoghurt." Viili is a very old culture of traditional yogurt, passed down through families and among friends in Finland for centuries. It is beloved for its many benefits, for its flavor, and because it is so easy to make. Each time yogurt is made, a small amount of the finished yogurt is simply kept aside to "inoculate" or "start" the next batch. In this way, families have fed themselves self-reliantly for thousands of years.

THE HISTORY OF VIILI
FINNISH YOGURT

The earliest known viili to come to the USA from Finland arrived in about 1900 with the Kinnunen family, who lived in Fort Bragg, northern California. It was popular in the Finnish community there," write William Shurtleff and Akiko Aoyagi in the book *History of Soy Yogurt, Soy Acidophilus Milk and Other Cultured Soy-milks*.[2] The culture remained in this small circle of people for the next eighty years, until the son of a Finnish immigrant living there offered the culture for sale in 1980.

Today, viili has begun to grow in popularity because more people are becoming aware of the health benefits of cultured foods.

There are two kinds of viili cultures. One is the ropy traditional viili, and the other is a creamy, smooth culture. The difference between the two cultures is that in ropy viili, natural wild yeasts have colonized. The traditional Finnish viili was ropy and stringy—when you put a spoon into it, you could stretch or pull ropes of yogurt out of the bowl. These ropes could be several inches long or even longer. However, many people don't consider this sort of slimy yogurt as appetizing

> ANY VIILI YOGURT STARTER CAN BECOME ROPY OVER TIME IF YOU CONSISTENTLY KEEP MORE THAN A TABLESPOON OF THE FINISHED YOGURT AS YOUR STARTER FOR A NEW BATCH. THIS ALLOWS THE NATURAL YEASTS TO COLONIZE MORE STRONGLY OVER TIME. TO KEEP YOUR YOGURT CREAMY, USE ONLY A SMALL RESIDUE OF FINISHED YOGURT AS YOUR STARTER.

as the creamy variety. The invention of the microscope meant that the natural yeasts, which caused the ropiness, could be separated from the beneficial bacteria, making a viili culture that is creamy and smooth.[3] It is this culture that is preferred and sold today.

Throughout the centuries, there has also been a third kind of viili made in Finland. Cream viili, called *kermaviili*, is made from cream instead of milk and is used in cooking like sour cream; with dill, chives, and other spices as cold sauce for fish; and as a base for dip sauces.

WHAT IS PERPETUAL YOGURT?

ny yogurt that can be created forever from a "start" is called a perpetual yogurt. There are three types of yogurt in the world:

1 No-cook yogurt created from a start

2 Cooked yogurt created from a start

3 Yogurt that must be cooked, from a start, with rennet (an enzyme used to make cheese)

Viili is the only no-cook yogurt I know of in the world. Most yogurts fall into the second category. Icelandic skyr yogurt, which must be cooked and must have a start and rennet, is an example of the third category of yogurt.

Notes

1. *Adnan Tamime, ed.,* Fermented Milks *(Singapore: Blackwell Science Ltd, 2006).*
2. *William Shurtleff and Akiko Aoyagi, comps.,* History of Soy Yogurt, Soy Acidophilus Milk and Other Cultured Soymilks (1918–2012) *(Lafayette, CA: Soyinfo Center, 2012).*
3. *Ibid.*

WHY USE ViiLi?

There are lots of reasons to use viili, including the major health benefits I will detail in a moment. Viili is beloved because it is creamy—not sour, not zesty or tangy—and does not require cooking. It is the world's easiest yogurt!

- Viili is creamy, mild, and delicious.
- To my knowledge, viili is the only yogurt in the world that does not require cooking. Because of this, it is also the world's easiest yogurt to make.
- Viili is perpetual; once you have a culture, also called a "yogurt starter," you can use it for the rest of your life.
- Viili works with pasteurized milk (grocery store milk), raw milk, powdered milk, and goat's milk.
- Viili is Mother Nature's probiotic, turning milk into a

strongly probiotic yogurt treat filled with beneficial bacteria that support digestive health. (More on this in a moment.)

- Viili fits into the flow of a busy life. You can let it set up overnight. If you are not ready to eat it, you can keep it in the fridge. If you need to take a break, your yogurt starter will wait in the fridge for you, even for months. Vacations, family emergencies, a busy schedule—whatever is going on in your life, viili tolerates benign neglect. This is why it has been a Scandinavian staple food for as far as memory stretches back.

HEALTH BENEFITS OF VIILI FINNISH YOGURT

- Viili yogurt, when in our gut, produces enzymes that hydrolyze the food we eat. "Hydrolysis" means that complex compounds are broken down so that they are more easily used by the body.[1]
- Viili breaks down lactose and predigests milk proteins, so that instead of irritating the digestive tract, the lactose and proteins can be digested.[2]
- Viili's natural fermentation hydrolyzes other milk proteins

that cause milk allergies in some people, making the proteins harmless.[3]

- Viili increases the content of B vitamins in dairy products.[4]
- Viili increases human absorption of the natural calcium and iron in milk.[5]
- Viili inhibits the growth of pathogenic microorganisms in the human digestive tract. This means that the good bacteria and yeasts are protected and the bad bacteria and yeasts are controlled or destroyed. Repeated scientific studies have shown the competitive abilities of kefir and viili to inhibit bad bacterial growth in the human gut![6]
- Viili "inhibits the action of some cancers."[7]
- Viili decreases cholesterol levels in the blood.[8, 9, 10]
- Viili boosts and regulates the human immune system.[11]
- Viili inhibits tumor growth in the human body.[12]
- Viili allows beneficial bacteria to better adhere to and survive the human digestive tract, which allows for continuity of beneficial bacteria in the digestive tract.[13]

Notes

1. *Y. H. Hui and E. Özgül Evranuz, et al., eds.,* Handbook of Animal-Based Fermented Food and Beverage Technology, *2nd ed. (Boca Raton, FL: CRC Press, 2012).*

2. *Ibid.*

3. *Jeremija Lj Rašić and Joseph A. Kurmann,* Yoghurt: Scientific Grounds, Technology, Manufacture and Preparations *(Copenhagen: Technical Dairy Publishing House, 1978).*

4. *H. Oberman and Z. Libudzisz, "Fermented Milks,"* in Microbiology of Fermented Foods, *ed. Brian J. B. Wood, 2nd ed., Vol. 1 (London: Blackie Academic & Professional, 1998).*

5. *Ibid.*

6. *Ibid.*

7. *Ibid.*

8. *Ibid.*

9. *Hajime Nakajima et al., "Cholesterol-lowering activity of ropy fermented milk,"* Journal of Food Science 57, no. 6 (1992): 1327–9.

10. *R. M. Pigeon et al., "Binding of free bile acids by cells of yogurt starter culture bacteria,"* Journal of Dairy Science 85, no. 11 (2002): 2705–10.

11. *Haruki Kitazawa et al., "B-cell mitogenic activity of slime products produced from slime-forming, encapsulated* Lactococcus lactis *ssp.* cremoris," Journal of Dairy Science 75, no. 11 (1992): 2946–51.

12. *Sylvie Chabot et al., "Exopolysaccharides from* Lactobacillus rhamnosus *RW-9595M stimulate TNF, IL-6 and IL-12 in human and mouse cultured immunocompetent cells, and IFN-γ in mouse splenocytes,"* Le Lait 81, no. 6 (2001): 683–697.

13. *Patricia Ruas-Madiedo et al., "Short communication: effect of exopolysaccharide isolated from 'viili' on the adhesion of probiotics and pathogens to intestinal mucus,"* Journal of Dairy Science 89, no. 7 (2006): 2355–8.

HOW TO GET "STARTED"

eedRenaissance.com is the world's only source for a dried viili yogurt starter culture kit. This kit arrives in the mail with flakes of dried yogurt and instructions for rehydrating the flakes in milk. Once your dried flakes have produced fresh yogurt, you can use a small amount (one teaspoon or less) of fresh yogurt as your yogurt starter from then on. Each time you have a finished batch of yogurt, simply reserve one teaspoon or the residue of the yogurt in your jar or container. This way, you never need another starter again and you will be able to make yogurt for the rest of your life.

You may also keep a small amount of finished yogurt in the fridge as a backup. It can be important to keep a backup because—as I have heard from many people who have used viili—the idea that residue in a jar can be valuable and important isn't always obvious to the modern mind. Because of this, viili starters are sometimes thrown away by spouses or family members who believe they are clearing out the fridge.

"WAKING UP" YOUR DRIED YOGURT CULTURE

Anyone can easily make mild, creamy viili yogurt. All you need is a start of this particular strain. (A culture, also called a "start," is simply a portion of the finished yogurt.) Dried starters are available at SeedRenaissance.com. To find them, click on the "Yeast & Cultures" category. You can also use a fresh culture, if you are lucky enough to know someone who is already making viili.

Keep in mind that viili is a particular mixed strain of natural, beneficial bacteria. Viili is not sold in any grocery store in the United States and is not available commercially in the United States. To make it, you must have a culture specifically for viili. Trying to use yogurt from the grocery store will not work for creating viili perpetual no-cook yogurt.

Dried starts and fresh starts are used differently. SeedRenaissance.com is the only source of dried viili yogurt cultures in the world. These cultures have not been freeze dried or modified. The dried starter packet will contain either one large flake or several smaller flakes of starter that have been dried using a proprietary method. Even though the amount of flakes in your starter kit may not seem like much, you can reserve half of your dried flake(s) as a backup if you wish.

To get "started" for the first time, put your dried culture flake(s) into 1/2 cup of milk (pasteurized or raw) in a glass jar. Loosely close the jar with a lid. Put the jar on your kitchen counter, on top of your fridge, or in a sunny window. Leave the jar until the milk has turned into yogurt. Because the dried starter must "wake up" and come to life, this will take one to three days. The first time you do this from a dried start, it will take much longer than using a fresh start would, so don't be alarmed if it takes two to three days. DO NOT put the container in the fridge until the yogurt has formed, or it may never form. If it has been more than forty-eight hours and nothing is happening, it means your starter is too cold. Move it to a warmer location, like a sunny windowsill.

When the yogurt is formed, you may eat it immediately or refrigerate for two to three days. The yogurt stays mild and creamy if refrigerated soon after it has formed. You can tell the yogurt is finished by tipping the jar slightly to one side. If you can see the yogurt begin to peel away from the glass in a solid mass, it is ready to eat.

The yogurt will begin to go sour if left at room temperature after it has formed. See the next section for instructions if your yogurt has gone sour.

USING A LIVE CULTURE PERPETUALLY

Once you have created your first batch of yogurt from your dried start, making more yogurt is easy.

To continue the start, empty the glass jar containing the yogurt so that only a residue of yogurt remains in the bottom of the jar. Put in as much milk as you desire, and leave the jar out as described in the previous section until yogurt has formed. If you put in a small amount of milk (1–2 cups), it may take six to eight hours for new yogurt to form. If you put in half a gallon of milk, it may take overnight or even eighteen to twenty-four hours for the yogurt to form.

Repeat this step again and again to create more yogurt.

Remember that viili will slowly turn sour as it ages, even

if kept in the refrigerator. To avoid making sour yogurt, it is important that there is only yogurt residue left in the glass jar when you fill it with milk to make your new batch.

If your viili yogurt goes sour, discard the yogurt, leaving behind just the residue, and follow the previous instructions for fresh, mild yogurt. The residue, after being mixed with fresh milk, can be moved into a clean jar at any time. Viili Finnish yogurt should *not* be kept in the fridge until *after* the yogurt has fully formed because cold temperatures stop yogurt growth. If your life goes crazy, you can leave your viili in the fridge for weeks and then get it going again by throwing out all but the residue and adding milk.

Eat your yogurt plain or combined with fruit or other flavorings. You can use viili to replace some of the oil or butter in certain baking recipes; for smoothies, green smoothies, or medicinal smoothies; to make dips; and more. The recipes in this book range from quick bread to dinners, smoothies, and much more.

TİPS

- Do not stir or agitate the yogurt while it is forming. If the yogurt is jostled while setting up, it may never set up properly. If your live (not dried) viili starter has been stirred or moved and has not set up properly after forty-eight hours, take out a small portion and start again, discarding the remaining failed yogurt.

- For sanitary purposes, avoid touching your yogurt start with your hands. Always use clean utensils when handling or transferring a yogurt start.

- You can transfer your yogurt to a clean container each time you start a new batch, or you can use the same container to make several batches in succession. You should transfer your start to a clean container at least once a month, or more often if you are making a new batch every day or if your yogurt is often on the counter and not in the fridge. Yogurt is food and should be kept clean and sanitary at all times.

- Always keep your viili yogurt covered, whether with a lid or a breathable cloth or paper towel cover. When using a cloth or paper towel cover, secure the cover to the jar using a rubber band or other fastening device. Remember that the air in your home may have airborne pet hair, human hair, dust, or other air pollutants that can settle into your yogurt start if it is not kept covered.

- If your yogurt appears to be growing mold of any color, or if it is polluted with any kind of additive or object, discard the yogurt and get a fresh starter from SeedRenaissance. com.

MAKING THICKER VIILI FINNISH YOGURT

- Instead of using a lid on your jar of yogurt, use breathable fabric or a paper towel as the lid. This allows the yogurt to "breathe" and makes a noticeably thicker, firmer yogurt.
- Raw milk makes the creamiest, thickest yogurt.
- Yogurt is thickest at its peak of freshness, before it begins to sour. For the best yogurt, refrigerate as soon as it is done to keep it from souring.
- To make thick, Greek yogurt–like viili, follow the recipe in Part Two of this book.

QUESTIONS AND ANSWERS ABOUT VIILI

Q: Can I use viili to make green smoothies?

A: Yes! The health benefits of properly prepared green smoothies cannot be overstated. For green smoothies to be truly powerful for the body, use a base of natural viili Finnish yogurt. Viili contains a natural mix of beneficial probiotic bacteria and yeasts. Lactose intolerance is a problem for a growing number of people whose gut health has been compromised by the lack of a prebiotic and probiotic diet. Probiotics break down food, making it more available to the human digestive system. Without them, some of the nutrition we need, especially minerals and basic nutrients, passes through us instead of being taken up by the body.

Q: I read on the Internet that viili cannot be used with raw milk because the enzymes in raw milk overcome the yogurt culture over time.

A: Not true. Viili wouldn't exist without raw milk. Remember that pasteurized milk is a relatively new invention, and viili has been used for millennia. It was always used with raw milk, until pasteurization was invented, because that was the only choice.

Q: My viili is not forming. What am I doing wrong?

A: You are using the wrong kind of milk. I have successfully used viili with pasteurized milk, homogenized milk, raw cow's milk, and raw goat's milk. But some people have had trouble with milk from certain varieties of goats. If you are using raw goat's milk to make yogurt and your viili is not forming correctly, switch to another milk source (whole milk from the grocery store, for example). Remember that viili must use real milk—not coconut milk, soy milk, or other milk substitutes.

Q: I have used grocery store yogurt as a culture before, but the culture is only viable for a few uses before it peters out and won't make yogurt any more. Will my Seed Renaissance viili starter also peter out, forcing me to buy a new starter every few batches? Does the viili start eventually go bad or become contaminated or slowly die off or change?

A: No—and this is easy to prove. If it did, then viili simply wouldn't exist. The only source for viili that has ever existed is viili yogurt. Reserving some yogurt to use to start your next batch is the only way viili has been made, ever. There is no "mother source" or company or manufacturer to go to if you want a "virgin" start. If viili went bad or changed, it simply wouldn't exist anymore. But it has been used for centuries, always from a starter. Viili is perpetual. As long as you use it at least every few months and store it in the fridge when not in use, you will be able to use your viili starter for the rest of your life!

Q: Can the milk I use be cold, straight from the fridge, or does it need to be room temperature?

A: Cold milk works great—no need to let the milk sit out before mixing it into the viili starter.

Q: Are you sure viili works with raw milk? Have you tried it? Is raw milk legal where you live?

A: Yes, I have used both raw milk and pasteurized milk with viili many, many times. Raw milk has been legal for about three years where I live and is now available in stores. I prefer viili with raw milk because it is thicker and creamier, but because raw milk is expensive, I use pasteurized milk more often. I have also purchased raw goat's milk from a local farmer and used it successfully to make viili.

Q: Can I make viili Finnish yogurt with powdered milk? Whole milk? Skim milk? Goat's milk? Soy milk, cream, half-and-half, almond milk, coconut milk, cashew milk (or any other milk or milk substitute you can think of)?

A: I have successfully made viili using powdered milk, whole milk from the grocery store, and raw milk. Traditionally, viili was made with goat's milk. Raw milk makes the thickest, creamiest yogurt, and you can make it with half-and-half and cream, too. Sometimes I add a bit of one of these (a tablespoon or two) to mine when making it, just to make it creamier. Most people use milk substitutes such as soy milk because they have a reaction to the lactose (lactic acid) naturally found in cow's milk. But viili breaks down that acid and renders it harmless, making viili a great alternative for people who suffer from lactose intolerance. Soy milk, almond milk, coconut milk, and other milk alternatives will not form viili yogurt successfully. If you have a favorite milk substitute that you prefer, experiment with the viili culture and see how it works! However, make sure you have a milk culture of viili to use as your perpetual start in case your experiment with milk substitutes fails.

Q: Is it possible to make a gallon of viili at a time? How much start would I need, and how long would that take?

A: You can make as much viili as you want, but the larger the amount, the longer it takes to turn into yogurt. To make a gallon at a time, I would use a half cup of starter (which is just a half cup of your previous yogurt), and it would probably be done overnight in my house with no air conditioning, but if you have cool air, it might take twenty-four to thirty-six hours (using a live start, not a dried start).

Q: Can I keep my yogurt in a metal container? Can I make it in a metal bowl?

A: No. As they begin to sour, all cultures (yeast, yogurt, kefir, etc.) produce natural acids that can interact with metal, giving the food a metallic taste. There are also concerns that stainless steel bowls made in China and other countries with fewer regulations may be mixed with impurities. If stainless steel is in fact diluted with cheaper metals, the acids in yogurts could dissolve those metals in small amounts. Whether or not this concern is substantiated or genuine, I don't know, but I never recommend that anyone keep yogurt in a metal container.

Q: Can I use a metal spoon to stir my yogurt? Can I use a metal spoon to eat my yogurt?

A: Yes. If you use a metal spoon to stir or eat your yogurt, the spoon is in contact with the yogurt for such a short amount of time that there should be no problems. Keep in mind that viili yogurt should never be stirred while it is setting up (turning to yogurt)—stirring actually breaks up the fragile curds, releasing the whey (clear liquid).

Q: My friend told me that homemade yogurt sets up better if I shake it every time I walk by it in the kitchen.

A: Your friend is incorrect. Yogurt should not be shaken or stirred because this damages the formation of the curd. Yogurt that is repeatedly disturbed while it is forming may never set a good curd.

Q: My viili has separated into a thick white portion and a clear portion. What did I do wrong?

A: Your viili has separated into curds and whey. This happens for one of two reasons: you may have left it at room temperature past its prime, or the yogurt may have been exposed to temperatures above 90 degrees while forming. Viili that has separated into curds and whey is almost always sour. If you shake the bottle (with the lid on), the curds and whey will mix back together. After shaking, discard all but the residue and start a new batch with the residue in the jar.

Q: You say to use only the residue in the jar, but my viili has formed a thick layer at the bottom of the jar that does not immediately pour out. Should I use this as my starter?

A: No. This thick layer may slowly turn your yogurt sour because it might contain more than a teaspoon of residue. To keep your yogurt mild, scrap most of this bottom layer out of the jar using a spatula and keep only a small bit of residue as your starter for the next batch of yogurt.

Q: My viili has a sparkling texture on the tongue, almost like carbonated soda. What am I doing wrong?

A: Viili can naturally produce carbonation in certain circumstances, especially when kept near a water kefir start, but this can occur even if you do not have a water kefir start. (Water kefir is another type of probiotic culture available at SeedRenaissance.com.) This carbonation occurs in viili yogurt most often if the yogurt formed too quickly because the ambient temperature was excessively hot or if the yogurt was left at room temperature too long after it finished forming. Carbonated yogurt is safe to eat (I actually enjoy it), but if you don't like it, simply discard the yogurt and leave residue to start a new batch.

Q: Can I store my residue in the fridge, or do I need to store only my finished yogurt in the fridge?

A: I often prefer to just store the residue in the empty jar in the fridge, especially if I am going on vacation or I am going to be out of town for a week or two. Storing just the residue means I can eat the finished yogurt, put the almost-empty jar in the fridge, and then start a fresh batch of yogurt once I am home again or when my schedule has calmed down to a dull roar.

Q: What if I am in a hurry and I need yogurt fast? Can I use a larger portion of yogurt as the culture in my milk to hurry the process?

A: When I teach classes on viili yogurt, students have told me that they were able to get their milk to turn to yogurt faster if they used more starter—1/2 cup of starter to 2 cups of milk. Keep in mind that "faster" in the language of starters means six hours instead of overnight. There is no "instant" way to make yogurt. However, keep in mind that if you put in this much starter every time, some percentage of your starter is getting older and older because you are always reserving so much starter each time and the old yogurt mixes with the new yogurt. Over time, your yogurt is likely to go sour because you are reserving so much starter.

Q: Can I put my viili in the oven with the light on to encourage it to make yogurt faster?

A: Possibly. However, you run the risk of spilling yogurt in the oven, or forgetting it is there, or having someone in your home turn the oven on and bake your yogurt. I have experimented with cooking milk mixed with viili starter to see how that works, but the yogurt never sets. I always keep my yogurt on the top of the fridge overnight and put it in the fridge in the morning if I don't use it immediately. Trying too hard to speed up Mother Nature is not likely to have good long-term results.

Q: My viili is delicious and easy to make, but it is not as thick as the yogurt from the grocery store. Why?

A: Yogurt from the grocery store often contains pectin, the same substance added to thicken jams and jellies. Grocery store yogurt also contains a large amount of sugar, which creates a very firm yogurt when combined with pectin. Viili, on the other hand, has no additives at all and is 100 percent natural. If you want thicker, firmer viili, use the recipe in Part Two of this book for Greek-style viili yogurt.

Q: Help! We are going on vacation for three weeks. What do I do with my viili?

A: Put a lid on your jar of yogurt, put it in the fridge, and leave it there until you come back. Viili will slowly go sour in the fridge but can still be used as a culture. When you get back, take a teaspoonful from the jar in the fridge and mix it with milk to start a fresh batch of yogurt on your counter-top, following the directions explained in this book. I have tested viili by leaving it in the fridge for up to six months, and it still makes great yogurt. Viili that has been in the fridge for months will slowly begin to oxidize, turning yellow and watery. The jar will smell sour when you open it; this is normal. However, if there is any kind of mold growing in the jar, discard the yogurt and get a fresh viili yogurt start at SeedRenaissance.com.

Q: Help! My viili is sour, even when I start a new culture. Why is it sour, and what can I do to make it normal again?

A: This is happening because you are leaving too much residue as your starter after a batch is finished. Use literally only the residue. A tiny amount of finished viili yogurt is all that you need to start a new batch with fresh milk. Remember also that your viili will begin to turn sour as soon as the yogurt has finished forming. If you are making only a pint of yogurt and leaving it to set up overnight, then try making a quart of yogurt instead. This larger amount of milk will take longer to form yogurt, and the longer time might be all you need to keep your yogurt from beginning to sour overnight on the counter. Remember also to put your viili in the fridge immediately after the yogurt has formed. This will retard the growth of the beneficial bacteria in the yogurt, keeping it from souring.

If you have a question that is not answered by a careful reading of this book, email me at calebwarnock@ yahoo.com. Please keep in mind that I often get hundreds of emails a day because my email address is in all of my books, and please ask only one question per email. If your question is vague or does not contain enough information, I cannot respond to ask for more details. Thank you for your understanding. If you do come up with a question I have not heard before, I will add your question to the viili-making instructions at SeedRenaissance.com.

PART TWO

RECIPES

YOGURTS AND CHEESES

VANILLA VIILI YOGURT

Makes 1 cup

1 cup (approximately) viili
  yogurt, chilled
4 drops vanilla extract

1 measured smidgen of
  powdered stevia extract,
  95% strength (available at
  SeedRenaissance.com), or
  honey to taste

Stir all ingredients together.

Serve chilled.

What is stevia? Stevia is an herb plant native to South America that has a naturally sweet leaf that contains no sugar and is very healthy. For full information, see my book *The Stevia Solution Cookbook* (Sanger, CA: Familius, 2016).

GREEK-STYLE VIILI YOGURT (VANILLA OR PLAIN)

Makes 4 cups

2 teaspoons unsweetened, unflavored gelatin powder (I use Knox)

1/2 cup whole milk
3 1/2 cups viili yogurt*

FOR VANILLA YOGURT:

1/4 teaspoon vanilla extract

1/8 teaspoon powdered stevia extract, 95 percent strength (available at SeedRenaissance.com)

*Viili yogurt is 99 percent lactose-free, which is one reason people use and eat it. If you are concerned about adding milk to this recipe, substitute the whey left over from making viili cheese (see page 44).

 Stir the gelatin powder into the milk.

2. Pour this mixture into a heavy-bottom saucepan and turn on the lowest heat. Stir every 30 seconds until the mixture is smooth without gelatin lumps. When the milk begins to boil (it will be a foam boil), turn off the heat.

3. Pour the viili yogurt into a medium bowl. Whisking the yogurt slowly, gradually drizzle in the heated milk mixture. Whisk a few more seconds.

4. For vanilla yogurt, stir in vanilla extract and stevia extract.

5. Put the whole bowl into the fridge for 1–2 hours until the yogurt has set up and is solid. Serve chilled.

VIILI FRUIT PARFAIT

Makes 1 serving

*1 cup vanilla viili yogurt,
chilled (see page 39)*
*1/4 cup of your favorite gra-
nola*

*Fresh, frozen, or dried fruit, to
taste (I prefer raspberries)*

Layer ingredients in a dish and serve.

VIILI SOFT CHEESE

Makes about 4 ounces of cheese; recipe can be doubled or quadrupled

*1 quart viili yogurt (chilled or
room temperature)*

Pinch of salt

Pour the yogurt into a flat-bottom saucepan. Stir in
the salt. Put the pan on the lowest possible heat. Stir
only occasionally, about once a minute. Within a few
minutes, the yogurt will begin to separate into curds
and whey in the pan. As soon as you see that chunks
of curd have formed, turn off the heat.

2   Position a strainer over a bowl. Line the strainer with a reusable sieve cloth (available at SeedRenaissance.com) or cheesecloth. Pour the heated yogurt from the pan into the lined strainer. Allow the whey to drain out into the bowl below the strainer (this takes about 1 minute). The cheese curd will stay in the cloth.

3   Squeeze the curd in the cloth, or press it with the back of a spoon, to remove as much whey as possible. Serve immediately.

4   For later use, put several ice cubes in the warm whey and stir until they melt. Put the ball of soft cheese in the whey and put the bowl in the fridge. Use within 3 days.

VIILI FIRM (GRATABLE) CHEESE

Makes about 4 ounces of cheese; recipe can be doubled or quadrupled

1 quart viili yogurt (chilled or   Pinch of salt
room temperature)

1. Pour the yogurt into a flat-bottom saucepan. Stir in the salt. Put the pan on the lowest possible heat. Stir only occasionally, about once a minute. Within a few minutes, the yogurt will begin to separate into curds and whey in the pan. As soon as you see that chunks of curd have formed, turn off the heat.

2. Position a strainer over a bowl. Line the strainer with a reusable sieve cloth (available at SeedRenaissance.com) or cheesecloth. Pour the heated yogurt from the pan into the lined strainer. Allow the whey to drain out into the bowl below the strainer (takes about 1 minute). The cheese curd will stay in the cloth.

3. Squeeze the curd in the cloth, or press it with the

back of a spoon, to remove as much whey as possible. Knead the curd several times.

 Put the curd in a bowl or container and chill in the fridge until the curd is firm. Store in a covered container and use within 3–4 days.

SMOOTHIES AND FROZEN TREATS

CANTALOUPE BANANA SMOOTHIE OR CREAMY FROZEN TREAT

Makes approximately 3 cups

1 cup viili yogurt
2 measured pinches powdered
    stevia extract, 95 percent
    strength (available at
    SeedRenaissance.com)
1 banana, peeled
1/2 organic apple, cored (I
    leave the skin on, but this is
    optional)

1 cup diced cantaloupe, fresh
    or frozen (1 cup is roughly
    1/4 of a fresh cantaloupe,
    peeled and deseeded)
3 ice cubes, or 1/4 cup crushed
    ice

FOR A SMOOTHIE:

1–2 tablespoons protein powder
1/4 cup ice or more depending on personal preference

Extra stevia, added by half pinches to make the smoothie sweeter

1   Combine all ingredients in a blender and blend until smooth. For a smoothie, serve immediately.

2   If making a creamsicle or frozen pop, pour the blended mixture into a frozen treat mold and freeze for 1–2 hours until solid.

MANGO APPLE SMOOTHIE
OR CREAMY FROZEN TREAT

Makes approximately 3 cups

1 cup viili yogurt
2 measured pinches powdered
  stevia extract, 95 percent
  strength (available at
  SeedRenaissance.com)
1/2 organic apple, cored (I
  leave the skin on, but this is
  optional)

1 cup mango, cubed, fresh or
  frozen
1 cup diced cantaloupe, fresh
  or frozen (1 cup is roughly
  1/4 of a fresh cantaloupe,
  peeled and deseeded)
3 ice cubes, or 1/4 cup crushed
  ice

FOR A SMOOTHIE:

1–2 tablespoons protein
  powder
1/4 cup ice or more depending
  on personal preference

Extra stevia, added by half
  pinches to make the smoothie sweeter

1   Combine all ingredients in a blender and blend until
    smooth. For a smoothie, serve immediately.

2   If making a creamsicle or frozen pop, pour the blend-
    ed mixture into a frozen treat mold and freeze for 1–2
    hours until solid.

CREAMY WATERMELON SMOOTHIE OR FROZEN TREAT

Makes approximately 4 cups

1 cup viili yogurt
3 measured pinches powdered stevia extract, 90 percent strength (available at SeedRenaissance.com)

4 cups fresh watermelon, cubed
6 ice cubes, or 1/2 cup crushed ice

FOR A SMOOTHIE:

1–2 tablespoons protein powder
1/4 cup ice or more depending on personal preference

Extra stevia, added by half pinches to make the smoothie sweeter

1   Combine all ingredients in a blender and blend until smooth. For a smoothie, serve immediately.

2   If making a creamsicle or frozen pop, pour the blended mixture into a frozen treat mold and freeze for 1–2 hours until solid.

PUMPKIN PIE SMOOTHIE

Makes 3 cups

2 cups vanilla viili yogurt (see page 39)
1/4 teaspoon cinnamon
1/8 teaspoon nutmeg

1 cup pumpkin puree (not pumpkin pie filling, which has sugar and other ingredients added)
Pinch of ground clove or allspice

OPTIONAL:

Substitute all spices in this recipe with 1/3 teaspoon pumpkin pie spice

1   Using a blender, combine and puree all ingredients until the mixture is smooth with no lumps of pumpkin puree.

2   Serve chilled. Top with crumbled graham crackers if desired.

BERRY PIE SMOOTHIE

Makes 3 cups

2 cups vanilla viili yogurt (see page 39)

1 cup raspberries, strawberries, blackberries, blueberries, or a mixture of berries

1   Using a blender, combine and puree all ingredients until the mixture is smooth with no lumps of berries.

2   Serve chilled. Top with crumbled graham crackers if desired.

PEACH SMOOTHIE

Makes 2 cups

2 cups vanilla viili yogurt (see page 39)

1 ripe peach, or 1 cup of diced bottled peaches

1. Using a blender, combine and puree all ingredients until the mixture is smooth with no lumps of peaches.

2. Serve chilled. Top with crumbled graham crackers if desired.

DRESSINGS

VIILI HOMEMADE RANCH DRESSING

Makes 2 cups

1 1/2 cups viili yogurt
1 small clove garlic, or 1/2
   teaspoon garlic granules or
   powder
1/4 teaspoon salt
1/4 teaspoon black pepper
1/2 teaspoon vinegar
1/4 cup parsley, dried or fresh

1–2 tablespoons dill, dried or
   fresh
1 tablespoon chives
1/4 teaspoon paprika
1/8 teaspoon cayenne pepper
1 teaspoon Worcestershire
   sauce

 Combine all ingredients in a blender. Blend until smooth. (If you want to make the dressing thicker, add 1–2 teaspoons oatmeal flour, cornstarch, arrowroot, or flour.)

Refrigerate 4 hours or overnight, or refrigerate 24 hours for the best flavor.

CREAMY ITALIAN DRESSING

Makes 1 1/2 cups

1 1/2 cups viili yogurt
1 teaspoon Italian seasoning
  blend
1/2 teaspoon garlic powder

1/8 teaspoon ground black
  pepper
Salt to taste

 Stir all ingredients together in a bowl.

 Use immediately, or cover and chill for up to 1 week.

DIPS, DRESSINGS, AND TOPPINGS

Follow the packet directions, substituting viili for mayonnaise or sour cream. You can do this when making:

- Baked potato toppings
- Mashed potatoes
- Egg salad

ENTRÉES

CURRIED WALDORF PECAN SALAD

Serves 4

1/2 cup pecans, coarsely chopped, or 1/2 cup walnuts, coarsely chopped*

1 tablespoon mild curry powder

1 cup viili yogurt

1 pound cooked chicken, shredded

1 green apple, chopped

2 cups cooked brown rice (or white rice, quinoa, wheat berries, etc.)

2 celery ribs, chopped (or Swiss chard ribs, which is what I usually use)

6 dried apricot halves, chopped

1/4 cup chopped red onion (optional)

*Waldorf salad is usually made with walnuts, but walnuts give me canker sores, so I prefer pecans. You can use walnuts if you please.

1. Lightly toast the pecans in a frying pan for 3–5 minutes. In the last minute, add the curry powder to the pan to roast as well.

2. Let cool. Combine with the rest of the ingredients and serve.

YOGURT SLAW SALAD

Makes 2 serving(s)

1/2 cup vanilla viili yogurt (see page 39)

1 tablespoon apple cider vinegar

1 tablespoon Dijon mustard

1 teaspoon smoked paprika

1 teaspoon kosher salt

1/2 teaspoon ground black pepper

1 bag coleslaw mix, or 3 cups shredded cabbage plus 1 cup shredded carrots

1 cup apple chunks (optional)

Whisk together all liquid ingredients and spices.

Toss the remaining ingredients with the liquid and spice ingredients. Serve chilled.

GALILEE MEDITERRANEAN COLD YOGURT SOUP

Makes four 1-cup servings

3 cups viili yogurt, chilled
1 large tomato, diced
1/2 cup fresh cucumber, cut
   into 1/4-inch cubes
1/2 cup grated or cubed
   zucchini, or 1/2 cup other
   summer squash
2 radishes, diced or shredded
2 tablespoons diced onion
1 tablespoon chopped fresh
   dill

1 tablespoon chopped fresh
   mint
1/8 teaspoon salt
1/4 teaspoon freshly ground
   black pepper
1/3 cup crumbled viili firm
   cheese (see page 44)
2 teaspoons extra-virgin olive
   oil, for garnish
Grated zucchini or cucumber,
   for garnish

1   Slightly whisk the yogurt.

2   Stir in all ingredients except the olive oil and garnish-
   es. Cover and chill in the fridge for 1 hour or up to 2
   days.

3   Spoon the soup into four serving bowls. Top each
   bowl with 1/2 teaspoon olive oil and a sprinkling of
   grated zucchini or cucumber.

VIILI CILANTRO LIME MARINADE (FOR CHICKEN OR PORK)

Makes approximately 1 1/2 cups

1 cup viili yogurt

2–3 tablespoons chopped fresh cilantro

2 cloves garlic, minced, or 1 teaspoon garlic granules or powder

Zest and juice of 1 lime

1 tablespoon extra-virgin olive oil

1 teaspoon salt

1/2 teaspoon white or black pepper

> MY FAVORITE WAY TO USE THIS RECIPE IS TO MARINADE TENDERIZED PORK CHOPS FOR SEVERAL HOURS IN THE FRIDGE AND THEN BREAD THEM, USING THE MARINADE AS A COATING FOR THE BREAD CRUMBS. I THEN PAN-FRY THEM IN A BIT OF OIL.

1. First, put the yogurt in a blender. Then add the rest of the ingredients and blend until smooth.

2. Use this as a marinade for chicken or pork chops or as a coating before putting on panko bread crumbs. Cook and serve.

ZUCCHINI RAITA

Serves 4

1 teaspoon garam masala
1 teaspoon ground cumin
3 small zucchini or cucumbers (1 pound), halved and deseeded, or a mixture of zucchini and cucumbers

1 cup viili yogurt
1/4 cup chopped cilantro
1 tablespoon lime juice
1/4 teaspoon salt

1   Toast the garam masala and cumin in a frying pan for about 90 seconds until fragrant. Set aside to cool.

2   Grate the zucchini or cucumbers. Squeeze them dry and put them in a bowl.

3   Stir in the remaining ingredients, including the roasted spices. Chill and serve.

STUFFED TOMATOES

4 large tomatoes
1/2 cup viili yogurt
1 cup shredded cooked chicken
1/4 cup pine nuts
1/4 cup diced Swiss cheese, or
    1/4 cup viili cheese, soft or
    firm (see page 42 or 41)
1/4 cup shredded carrots
1/4 cup shredded beets
2 celery stalks, sliced, or 2
    Swiss chard stalks, sliced
1 tablespoon finely chopped
    onion, or 2 sliced green
    onions

2 tablespoons chopped fresh
    basil
Juice of half a lemon
1 teaspoon curry powder, or 1
    teaspoon garam masala
2 large tomatoes, deseeded
    and diced
Salt and black pepper to taste
1/2 cup cooked garbanzo
    beans (optional)
1/2 teaspoon chopped fresh
    savory (optional)
Shredded carrots or beets, for
    garnish

1   Cut off the tops of the 4 large tomatoes. Scoop out
    and discard the insides.

2   In a bowl, stir all remaining ingredients except the
    garnishes together until just incorporated. Fill the
    tomatoes with the mixture.

3   Top with shredded carrots or beets and serve chilled.

DESSERTS

BERRY YOGURT PIE

2 teaspoons unsweetened,
  unflavored gelatin powder (I
  use Knox)
1/2 cup whole milk*
3 1/2 cups viili yogurt
1/4 teaspoon vanilla extract
1/8 teaspoon powdered stevia
  extract, 95 percent strength
  (available at
  SeedRenaissance.com)

1 cup fresh or frozen berries
  (raspberries, strawberries,
  blackberries, blueberries, or
  a mix of berries)
1/3 cup coconut palm sugar (or
  other sugar)
1/4 cup lemon juice
Finely grated zest of 1 lemon
1 prepared graham cracker
  piecrust

1 Stir the gelatin powder into the milk.

2 Pour this mixture into a heavy-bottom saucepan and
turn on lowest heat. Stir every 30 seconds until the
mixture is smooth without gelatin lumps. When the

milk beings to boil (it will be a foam boil), turn off the heat.

3. Pour the yogurt into a medium bowl. Whisking the yogurt vigorously, slowly drizzle in the heated milk mixture as you whisk. Whisk a few more seconds.

4. Put the whole bowl into the fridge for 1–2 hours until the yogurt has set up and is solid.

5. Combine the berries with the coconut palm sugar, lemon juice, and lemon zest in a saucepan. Bring to a boil over medium heat.

6. Turn off heat, cool, and refrigerate. Use this berry mixture to top the yogurt pie.

YOGURT WAFFLES

1 cup whole wheat flour (or flour of your choice, or natural yeast)
1 teaspoon baking powder
1/2 teaspoon salt
1 egg

1 cup viili yogurt
2 tablespoons melted butter
1 tablespoon oil of your choice (vegetable, olive, coconut, or other cooking oil)

1   Whisk dry ingredients together.

2   In a separate bowl, whisk wet ingredients together.

3   Pour wet ingredients into dry ingredients and whisk until just incorporated.

4   Coat a waffle iron with spray cooking oil. Slowly pour in the amount of batter recommended for your machine and cook for the suggested time.

5   Serve warm.

YOGURT PANCAKES

Makes 9–10 small pancakes

1 cup whole wheat flour (or flour of your choice, or natural yeast)
1 teaspoon baking powder
1/2 teaspoon salt

1 egg
1 cup viili yogurt
2 tablespoons melted butter
1/2 teaspoon honey or molasses

1   Whisk dry ingredients together.

2   In a separate bowl, whisk wet ingredients together.

3   Pour wet ingredients into dry ingredients and whisk until just incorporated.

4   Coat a frying pan or cooking surface with spray cooking oil or with a pat of butter. Slowly pour the batter into the pan until the pancake is your desired size. With the heat on medium low, brown the pancake on one side, then the other.

5   Serve warm.

ABOUT THE AUTHOR

Caleb Warnock is the bestselling author of fourteen books, including the popular *Forgotten Skills* series. He owns SeedRenaissance.com. He has a master's degree in English composition and has won more than two dozen awards for writing. Together with Kirsten Skirvin, he coauthored the book *Forgotten Skills of Backyard Herbal Healing and Family Health*. You can find all the episodes of Forgotten Skills Radio with Caleb Warnock at www.MormonHippie.com/category/forgotten-skills-radio/. Sign up for Caleb's newsletter on the bottom left-hand corner of SeedRenaissance.com. Caleb and his wife, Charmayne, live on the bench of the Rocky Mountains.

ABOUT FAMILIUS

Welcome to a place where mothers are celebrated, not compared. Where heart is at the center of our families, and family at the center of our homes. Where boo boos are still kissed, cake beaters are still licked, and mistakes are still okay. Welcome to a place where books—and family—are beautiful. Familius: a book publisher dedicated to helping families be happy.

VISIT OUR WEBSITE: WWW.FAMILIUS.COM

Our website is a different kind of place. Get inspired, read articles, discover books, watch videos, connect with our family experts, download books and apps and audiobooks, and along the way, discover how values and happy family life go together.

JOIN OUR FAMILY

There are lots of ways to connect with us! Subscribe to our newsletters at www.familius.com to receive uplifting daily inspiration, essays from our Pater Familius, a free ebook every month, and the first word on special discounts and Familius news.

BECOME AN EXPERT

Familius authors and other established writers interested in helping families be happy are invited to join our family and contribute online content. If you have something important to say on the family, join our expert community by applying at:

www.familius.com/apply-to-become-a-familius-expert

GET BULK DISCOUNTS

If you feel a few friends and family might benefit from what you've read, let us know and we'll be happy to provide you with quantity discounts. Simply email us at specialorders@familius. com.

Website: www.familius.com
Facebook: www.facebook.com/paterfamilius
Twitter: @familiustalk, @paterfamilius1
Pinterest: www.pinterest.com/familius

THE MOST IMPORTANT WORK YOU EVER DO WILL BE WITHIN THE WALLS OF YOUR OWN HOME.

CPSIA information can be obtained
at www.ICGtesting.com
Printed in the USA
FSOW01n2059050416
18857FS

9 781942 934516